NEW YORK REVIEW BOOKS
CLASSICS

WRITING POLITICS

DAVID BROMWICH is Sterling Professor of English at Yale University. His books include *Hazlitt: The Mind of a Critic*, *Disowned by Memory: Wordsworth's Poetry of the 1790s*, *The Intellectual Life of Edmund Burke*, and, most recently, *American Breakdown: The Trump Years and How They Befell Us*. His collection of essays on modern poetry, *Skeptical Music*, won the PEN/Diamonstein-Spielvogel Award for the Art of the Essay in 2002. His articles on contemporary politics, the war on terror, and the fate of civil liberties in the United States have appeared in *Dissent, The Nation, HuffPost, The New York Review of Books*, antiwar.com, *TomDispatch, Mondoweiss, Guernica*, and the *London Review of Books*.

WRITING POLITICS
An Anthology

Edited and with an introduction by
DAVID BROMWICH

NEW YORK REVIEW BOOKS

New York

THIS IS A NEW YORK REVIEW BOOK
PUBLISHED BY THE NEW YORK REVIEW OF BOOKS
435 Hudson Street, New York, NY 10014
www.nyrb.com

Library of Congress Cataloging-in-Publication Data
Names: Bromwich, David, 1951– editor.
Title: Writing politics : an anthology / edited by David Bromwich.
Description: New York : New York Review Books, [2020] | Includes
  bibliographical references.
Identifiers: LCCN 2020005812 (print) | LCCN 2020005813 (ebook) |
  ISBN 9781681374628 (paperback) | ISBN 9781681374635 (ebook)
Subjects: LCSH: Political science—History—Sources.
Classification: LCC JA83 .W75 2020 (print) | LCC JA83 (ebook) |
  DDC 320—dc23
LC record available at https://lccn.loc.gov/2020005812
LC ebook record available at https://lccn.loc.gov/2020005813

ISBN 978-1-68137-462-8
Available as an electronic book; ISBN 978-1-68137-463-5

Printed in the United States of America on acid-free paper.
10 9 8 7 6 5 4 3 2 1

CONTENTS

Introduction

THE POLITICAL essay has never been a clearly defined genre. David Hume may have legitimated it in 1758 when he classified under a collective rubric his own *Essays, Moral, Political, and Literary.* "Political," however, should have come last in order, since Hume took a speculative and detached view of politics, and seems to have been incapable of feeling passion for a political cause. We commonly associate political thought with full-scale treatises by philosophers of a different sort, whose understanding of politics was central to their account of human nature. Hobbes's *Leviathan*, Montesquieu's *Spirit of the Laws*, Rousseau's *Social Contract*, Mill's *Representative Government*, and, closer to our time, Rawls's *Theory of Justice*, all satisfy that expectation. What, then, is a political essay? By the late eighteenth century, the periodical writings of Steele, Swift, Goldsmith, and Johnson had broadened the scope of the English essay for serious purposes. The field of politics, as much as culture, appeared to their successors well suited to arguments on society and government.

A public act of praise, dissent, or original description may take on permanent value when it implicates concerns beyond the present moment. Where the issue is momentous, the commitment stirred by passion, and the writing strong enough, an essay may sink deep roots in the language of politics. An essay is an *attempt*, as the word implies— a trial of sense and persuasion, which any citizen may hazard in a society where people are free to speak their minds. A more restrictive idea of political argument—one that would confer special legitimacy on an elite caste of managers, consultants, and symbolic analysts— presumes an environment in which state papers justify decisions arrived at from a region above politics. By contrast, the absence of formal constraints or a settled audience for the essay means that the daily experience of the writer counts as evidence. A season of crisis tempts people to think politically; in the process, they sometimes discover reasons to back their convictions.

The experience of civic freedom and its discontents may lead the essayist to think beyond politics. In 1940, Virginia Woolf recalled the sound of German bombers circling overhead the night before; the insect-like irritant, with its promise of aggression, frightened her into thought: "It is a queer experience, lying in the dark and listening to the zoom of a hornet which may at any moment sting you to death." The ugly noise, for Woolf, signaled the prerogative of the fighting half of the species: Englishwomen "must lie weaponless tonight." Yet Englishmen would be called upon to destroy the menace; and she was not sorry for their help. The mood of the writer is poised between gratitude and a bewildered frustration. Woolf's essay, "Thoughts on Peace in an Air Raid," declines to exhibit the patriotic sentiment by which most reporters in her position would have felt drawn. At the same time, its personal emphasis keeps the author honest through the awareness of her own dependency.

Begin with an incident—*I could have been killed last night*—and you may end with speculations on human nature. Start with a national policy that you deplore, and it may take you back to the question, "Who are my neighbors?" In 1846, Henry David Thoreau was arrested for having refused to pay a poll tax; he made a lesson of his resistance two years later, when he saw the greed and dishonesty of the Mexican War: "Under a government which imprisons any unjustly, the true place for a just man is also a prison." But to Thoreau's surprise, the window of the prison had opened onto the life of the town he lived in, with its everyday errands and duties, its compromises and arrangements, and for him that glimpse was a revelation:

They were the voices of old burghers that I heard in the streets. I was an involuntary spectator and auditor of whatever was done and said in the kitchen of the adjacent village inn,—a wholly

new and rare experience to me. It was a closer view of my native
town. I was fairly inside of it. I had never seen its institutions
before. This is one of its peculiar institutions; for it is a shire
town. I began to comprehend what its inhabitants were about.

Slavery, at that time, was nicknamed "the peculiar institution," and
by calling the prison itself a peculiar institution, and maybe having
in mind the adjacent inn as well, Thoreau prods his reader to think
about the constraints that are a tacit condition of social life.

The *risk* of political writing may lure the citizen to write—a fact
Hazlitt seems to acknowledge in his essay "On the Regal Character,"
where his second sentence wonders if the essay will expose him to
prosecution: "In writing a criticism, we hope we shall not be accused
of intending a libel." (His friend Leigh Hunt had recently served two
years in prison for "seditious libel" of the Prince Regent—having
characterized him as a dandy notorious for his ostentation and obe-
sity.) The writer's consciousness of provocative intent may indeed be
inseparable from the wish to persuade; though the tone of commitment will vary with the zeal and composition of the audience, whether
that means a political party, a movement, a vanguard of the enlight-
ened, or "the people" at large. Edmund Burke, for example, writes to
the sheriffs of Bristol (and through them to the city's electors) in
order to warn against the suspension of habeas corpus by the British
war ministry in 1777. The sudden introduction of the repressive act,
he tells the electors, has imperiled their liberty even if they are for
the moment individually exempt. In response to the charge that the
Americans fighting for independence are an unrepresentative minor-
ity, he warns: "*General* rebellions and revolts of an whole people never
were *encouraged*, now or at any time. They are always *provoked*." So
too, Mahatma Gandhi addresses his movement of resistance against
British rule, as well as others who can be attracted to the cause, when
he explains why nonviolent protest requires courage of a higher degree
than the warrior's: "Non-violence is infinitely superior to violence,
forgiveness is more manly than punishment." In both cases, the writer
treats the immediate injustice as an occasion for broader strictures

on the nature of justice. There are certain duties that governors owe to the governed, and duties hardly less compulsory that the people owe to themselves.

Apparently diverse topics connect the essays that follow; but, taken loosely to illustrate a historical continuity, they show the changing face of oppression and violence, and the invention of new paths for improving justice. Arbitrary power is the enemy throughout—power that, by the nature of its asserted scope and authority, makes itself the judge of its own cause. King George III, whose reign spanned sixty years beginning in 1760, from the first was thought to have overextended monarchical power and prerogative, and by doing so to have reversed an understanding of parliamentary sovereignty that was tacitly recognized by his predecessors. Writing against the king, "Junius" (the pen name of Philip Francis) traced the monarch's errors to a poor education; and he gave an edge of deliberate effrontery to the attack on arbitrary power by addressing the king as *you*. "It is the misfortune of your life, and originally the cause of every reproach and distress, which has attended your government, that you should never have been acquainted with the language of truth, until you heard it in the complaints of your people." A similar frankness, without the ad hominem spur, can be felt in Burke's attack on the monarchical distrust of liberty at home as well as abroad: "If any ask me what a free Government is, I answer, that, for any practical purpose, it is what the people think so; and that they, and not I, are the natural, lawful, and competent judges of this matter." Writing in the same key from America, Thomas Paine, in his seventh number of *The Crisis*, gave a new description to the British attempt to preserve the unity of the empire by force of arms. He called it a war of conquest; and by addressing his warning directly "to the people of England," he reminded the king's subjects that war is always a social evil, for it sponsors a violence that does not terminate in itself. War enlarges every opportunity of vainglory—a malady familiar to monarchies.

The coming of democracy marks a turning point in modern discussions of sovereignty and the necessary protections of liberty. Confronted by the American annexation of parts of Mexico, in 1846–48,

Thoreau saw to his disgust that a war of conquest could also be a popular war, the will of the people directed to the oppression of persons. It follows that the state apparatus built by democracy is at best an equivocal ally of individual rights. Yet as Emerson would recognize in his lecture "The Fugitive Slave Law," and Frederick Douglass would confirm in "The Mission of the War," the massed power of the state is likewise the only vehicle powerful enough to destroy a system of oppression as inveterate as American slavery had become by the 1850s. Acceptance of political evil—a moral inertia that can corrupt the ablest of lawmakers—goes easily with the comforts of a society at peace where many are satisfied. "Here was the question," writes Emerson: "Are you for man and for the good of man; or are you for the hurt and harm of man? It was question whether man shall be treated as leather? whether the Negroes shall be as the Indians were in Spanish America, a piece of money?" Emerson wondered at the apostasy of Daniel Webster, *How came he there?* The answer was that Webster had deluded himself by projecting a possible right from serial compromise with wrong.

Two ways lie open to correct the popular will without a relapse into docile assent and the rule of oligarchy. You may widen the terms of discourse and action by enlarging the community of participants. Alternatively, you may strengthen the opportunities of dissent through acts of exemplary protest—protest in speech, in action, or both. Gandhi and Martin Luther King, Jr. remain the commanding instances in this regard. Both led movements that demanded of every adherent that the protest serve as an express image of the society it means to bring about. Nonviolent resistance accordingly involves a public disclosure of the work of conscience—a demonstrated willingness to make oneself an exemplary warrior without war. Because they were practical reformers, Gandhi and King, within the societies they sought to reform, were engaged in what Michael Oakeshott calls "the pursuit of intimations." They did not start from a model of the good society generated from outside. They built on existing practices of toleration, friendship, neighborly care, and respect for the dignity of strangers.

Nonviolent resistance, as a tactic of persuasion, aims to arouse an audience of the uncommitted by its show of discipline and civic responsibility. Well, but why not simply resist? Why show respect for the laws of a government you mean to change radically? Nonviolence, for Gandhi and King, was never merely a tactic, and there were moral as well as rhetorical reasons for their ethic of communal self-respect and self-command. Gandhi looked on the British empire as a commonwealth that had proved its ability to reform. King spoke with the authority of a native American, claiming the rights due to all Americans, and he evoked the ideals his countrymen often said they wished to live by. The stories the nation loved to tell of itself took pride in emancipation much more than pride in conquest and domination. "So," wrote King from the Birmingham City Jail, "I can urge men to obey the 1954 decision of the Supreme Court because it is morally right, and I can urge them to disobey segregation ordinances because they are morally wrong."

A subtler enemy of liberty than outright prejudice and violent oppression is the psychological push toward conformity. This internalized docility inhabits and may be said to dictate the costume of manners in a democracy. Because the rule of mass *opinion* serves as a practical substitute for the absolute authority that is no longer available, it exerts an enormous and hidden pressure. This dangerous "omnipotence of the majority," as Tocqueville called it, knows no power greater than itself; it resembles an absolute monarch in possessing neither the equipment nor the motive to render a judgment against itself. Toleration thus becomes a political value that requires as vigilant a defense as liberty. Minorities are marked not only by race, religion, and habits of association, but also by opinion. "It is easy to see," writes Walter Bagehot in "The Metaphysical Basis of Toleration," "that very many believers would persecute sceptics" if they were given the means, "and that very many sceptics would persecute believers." Bagehot has in mind religious belief, in particular, but the same intolerance operates when it is a question of penalizing a word, a gesture, a wrongly sympathetic or unsympathetic show of feeling by which a fellow citizen might claim to be offended. The